IF YOU WAKE UP, YOU CAN CHANGE IT!

BISHOP ALVIN FREEMAN

authorHOUSE®

AuthorHouse™
1663 Liberty Drive
Bloomington, IN 47403
www.authorhouse.com
Phone: 1 (800) 839-8640

Published by AuthorHouse 12/14/2018

ISBN: 978-1-5462-7252-6 (sc)
ISBN: 978-1-5462-7250-2 (hc)
ISBN: 978-1-5462-7251-9 (e)

Library of Congress Control Number: 2018914785

Print information available on the last page.

This book is printed on acid-free paper.

IS THERE A GOD?

My life hasn't been easy. Although with God's help, I'm conquering the hardest parts.

I'm reminded of the instance in the Bible regarding the lady with the issue of blood. In this story told in Matthew Chapter 9, the woman had been sick for 12 years. When the woman approached Jesus, she did so with "***NOW FAITH.***" She knew that she would be healed.

Just a *little* faith takes a person so far. In my life, I was forced backwards. I had to ask myself, how do I achieve this "***NOW FAITH?***" I'm in this empty room and I'm gathering my trials and all my tribulations. How do I find a way around the things that have kept me bound? I needed a breakthrough immediately!

In hindsight, the reality is there are mothers that are raising their children by themselves. Also, there are so many homeless people and countless amounts that are living in poverty. I was led to break my situation down further. I know for sure that the status of my life does not compare to others in terms of pain and suffering. Although, the mental stress was consuming enough to make me feel like I was no different than these people. I was these people. I AM these people.

I remember appearing to be a single parent even when there were two parents in the home. We were both working full time jobs to support our family and our lifestyle. However, there were times that our children needed both of their parents and I was the only one. Our children were not accustomed to having only one parent. Nevertheless, they endured it. I was completely overwhelmed. I've worked many jobs. Some of which are the jobs no one wants to do but being the parent that our children needed was the hardest position I've ever held. Honestly, when you have a spouse that totally checks out that's when you need the Lord to check in.

My mom used to advise me and still does constantly about raising children.

"Focus on your children and believe me your days will be good."

I was now learning firsthand what she meant. She trying to explain to me that issues that I was concerning myself with were irrelevant. Nothing can move forward unless your household is completely stable. We often make the obstacles more complex by worrying about things we have no control over. It did feel like the end of the world, but it was not. Single parents, there are many struggles, but God knows we can handle them, so we do.

During the chaos, we learn very quickly. Therefore, I adapted to going to school meetings, participating in all the kid's sports activities, and financially providing in order to maintain the lifestyle they were accustomed to. It was a tough journey. All my praises go to the Lord. I had to believe in my Father. I had to trust that I would make it through and that God would take care of me. I compare myself to the bleeding woman. My *"NOW FAITH"* in the Lord, allowed me to ascend on my journey with confidence. It gives me the skills to cope with each struggle.

Don't take back your prayers. Don't listen to the enemy. Listen to Jesus. He will never steer you wrong.

How do you know when God is speaking to you? You seek him diligently. You fast. You pray. One obstacle at a time. One day at a time and when you receive it you can move on to the next trial.

Remember, if you can wake up you can change it.

RELATIONSHIPS ETC....

Relationships are supposed to be a hole in one. This means that healthy relationships require constant work. From time to time you will find that some people have continued their relationships through the good and the bad things. Again, it takes work. It takes God.

How do I meet the people that I'm compatible with? How do I meet my soulmate? In Christian faith, it is believed that God has selected the right one for you.

"I've asked God to send me the right one," we say. Ask yourself. How many times have you taken the wrong turn? You cannot ask God for something and then take it back. We often get misled by the enemy. We let him direct us on things that appear to be good and are not. When you must question the relationship in your head, it may be a clear indication that it is not of God. Be prayerful and that will lead you to answers about your situation.

Relationships deal solely with perception. How do those you are in contact with perceive you? If you project negative energy toward people, you are likely to lose the respect of those people. This is another tool you have access to. Be mindful. As a God-fearing Christian, you must walk the walk and talk the talk. Display to others exactly how you want to be seen. Of course, the enemy is going to try to make you out to be the opposite of your TRUE position but follow your chosen course.

In my experience women are the hardest individuals to adapt in their relationships. They tend to carry all their emotions on their sleeves and it nearly always turns out badly. When women have been scorned, they often have the hardest time in future relationships. They carry the so called "ride or die spirit," diving right in. Women will meet someone they deem to be very likable and then disclose every single detail about their personal lives. This is opening way too quickly. As a man, I am no longer listening. Men want to hear the positive not the negative when they first meet a woman. Your first impression has to be on a positive one.

Dating in this world is nothing like the old days. Most people are already sexually active, especially older and divorced women. Many of these women have children; therefore, a man must weigh his options and do so very quickly. Some men aren't looking for a ready-made family. This is the only subject to that needs to be addressed on the first date. A woman sharing mental or physical abuse is not necessary. As the relationship progresses, he's going to figure that out anyway. There will be times when the door is open to share things like that. Be aware that the time is not from the very beginning. However, if the subject comes up you can't lie but your delivery is everything.

Last, do not present yourself as a victim. We all know that here were warnings that you didn't yield to. Instead, talk about how you overcame the obstacles from past relationships. Remember it's all about your timing! These things are not easy at all. It is very necessary to have a spiritual relationship with God because he is your guide to a healthy relationship. Just keep your faith entrusted in him.

GOD ARE YOU THERE?

The older we get the more we can see the equalities toward one another. For instance, look to the story of Job.

The book begins with a discussion regarding Job. "Perfect and upright" man who "feared God and eschewed evil" (Job 1:1). I noticed something interesting. In the first chapter of Job, the Bible speaks of children taking turns throwing parties at their various homes. This was before Satan's request from God. Job had children that were worldly. After every party, Job would send for his children. He would pray for them and offer up a burnt offering for each one of them. Ten children, ten burnt offerings. It's amazing that the more you try it seems like the worst it gets. Then question you ask is, **GOD ARE YOU THERE?**"

Job felt the need to pray, despite all that sins that his children committed. You would think that Satan would ask for God to give up the children first, not Job. The enemy is always after the strongest in the home. Job went on his passage prepared to lose everything, including his children. Sometimes when we are going through trials, it's training for what's to come. If you can't handle your current trial, he will come along with the answers to all of your prayers. Different levels come with bigger trials.

Job was very close to God. God was so close to him that Job's trials only maimed him but did not destroy him. Only you can let the enemy destroy or overtake you! Stop for a moment and then say to yourself, "it is what it is." This is simply not accepting your troubles as your destiny.

Job kids were idol worshipers. I believe Satan saw this as a household weakness. Household weakness is like a crack in a strong wall. It will eventually expand to take that wall right down. These cracks are called stress cracks. We get them in our house sometimes.

We also can call them," strongholds." The enemy wants to protect his means of attack on you. When we fast and pray, we can cast down every stronghold against us. In Matthew 17:21, Jesus said, "Howbeit this kind goeth not out but by prayer and fasting."

Suffering is a necessary and is normal to Christians. Suffering produces perseverance. Hang on in there.

Life says you can't, people say you can't, society says you can't, but you can make it through all obstacles. If you lost all that Job had, would you do what he did? Could you stand up in the middle of carnage and say, "though he slay me yet will I trust him?" Amazing isn't it! Of course, God is there!

"GOD IS NOT DONE WORKING ON ME"

Acts 9 talks about the conversation of Saul of Taurus (Paul)

Paul was a torturer and murderer of the Christians. Jesus stopped him in the middle of a trip to Damascus. When the light from the heavens shone on him, he was quickly stunned and afraid. Especially after hearing the voice of Jesus.

"Why are you persecuting the Saints of God?" He was immediately humbled by the voice of Jesus. At the time Paul was ready to do whatever it took to be obedient to Jesus. (Acts 9:3-4)

Paul asked, "what can I do Lord?" Paul was educated and gave thought to everything that was going on. Paul immediately took the chance to follow God! There was working to be done by Saul of Taurus.

The conversation was the beginning of his walk with Jesus. Our bad beginnings don't determine our destiny! We do! God provides the opportunity, but we must seize it ourselves. It is amazing what God has done for me as well. Taking me from very humble beginnings to where I am now. I've been poor, homeless and friendless. God kept and saved me like Saul was saved.

Being your worst out of ignorance is one thing, God can work with that, but having the knowledge and disregarding is totally different. When God gives it is important to be humble. One of the first gifts that God presented us with was the ability to communicate with him openly. The carnal mind is in enmity opposed against God: for it is not subject to the law of God, neither indeed can be. (Romans 8:7 KJV).

Endurance is very important! If you have been able to endure the trials of life you already have what it takes. Endurance means: the fact or power of enduring an unpleasant or difficult process or situation without giving way. This is so important for us in so many ways. For instance, a person running a marathon, that person wakes up daily to train for that race. They know in their mind they have to make it to the finish whether they win or lose. It's a great feeling to know that you completed the goals that you set for yourself. The result being you feel great about yourself and you feel complete.

God wants us to trust him in everything we do. Of course, there are times we doubt God. There are times when we're hard headed, by not listening and we feel ourselves repeating the same tasks over and over. Feeling like you've mastered this process is a mistake! Your walk with God is a constant journey. He's never done with you. Every second, minute, and hour he is dealing with us. Let's say, all day, every day.

God chose you, you must give your total soul to him. No doubts; just surrender. If I can do it, so can you.

SNAP OUT OF IT!

How many of us live in a fantasyland? Fantasyland is a place that is imaginary or that excites wonder. I am reminded of the story in the Bible about the prodigal son. The prodigal son is a character in a parable Jesus told to illustrate how generous God is when forgiving sinners who repent.

The prodigal son was the youngest of two sons. He asked for his inheritance and he left home for a far country. He lived wildly and could not maintain his wealth. He lost it all. When he came to his senses, he returned home to ask his father for forgiveness. The son was so humble at this point that he even asked to work as a servant.

When you realize you make mistake, you snap out of it! Point blank, period! We have people in this world that live a lavish lifestyle from day to day and know they can't afford it. We live beyond our means like it's all right. Eventually it runs out. This leads people to other levels of sin. How far will we go to keep up with this world? Some of us will do whatever we feel we have to do in order to live the fantasies we have created in our head. It's bad when you're forging checks, committing credit card fraud, and robbing. I can go on and on to describe what man will do just to live in the land of nowhere. Snap out of it!

As Christians we must be led differently. We must be humble. God has to guide us to be mindful and to understand how to receive all of the blessings that are right here for us to have. We need guidance that is spiritual and not of the world. There are people who have everything and still are not happy. We don't understand that most people that are wealthy, would trade it back just to have peace and be happy.

Being wealthy also requires being disciplined mentally when spending. We always ask for something from God that we have no knowledge of how to maintain. It's a sense of maturity one has to have to obtain anything of importance. Snap out of it!

It may be hard to accept that you need tools to be fruitful in everything that you do. My biggest tool is Christ. I've tried to maintain life alone it doesn't work, trust me. I've never had the opportunity to be reckless. I've had mentors throughout my life that took the time to show me the way. There were no handouts, and I was given nothing. I've had to work for everything I obtained in life. It was very hard to do.

The options for finding your way years ago were more negative than positive. I couldn't have my life taxed from a bad decision. I'm not saying I've done everything perfect, but I didn't want to have the fear of losing my soul plaguing me on a regular basis. The "snap out of it" is what we do when there is no more hope for the situation we're in. It becomes obvious.

The prodigal son had to "snap out of it" because he realized there were no more options for his life. If you are in a meaningless relationship, in a financial war, taking on the responsibilities of others, and not seeking our father for guidance, my advice for you is to SNAP OUT OF IT!

POWER!!!

How many of us need the power? I would say all of us. How many of us seek spiritual power? I want to say all of us.

"For God hath not given us the spirit of fear but of power and love and of a sound mind." (2 Timothy 1:7 KJV)

"But you shall receive power after the Holy Ghost is come upon you and you shall be Witnesses unto me both in Jerusalem, in all Judea, and Samaria and on to the uttermost part of the Earth. (Acts 1:8)

These two passages are dear to me, we have power even when we don't recognize it. God granted us that. Some of us use our powers for the wrong reasons. We have people in positions in the world that use power or authority to do their jobs. There are times when that power and authority is abused. We have to use the power that we have in the world to gain spiritual power which we receive from the Lord. We look to the politicians of this world and expect that they would do the right thing because of the positions held but that's not always so. Nowadays, we have to vote. In order to campaign, the world places one person against the next person. Then as citizens we must decide on who is going to lead us. In our mind, we automatically think that the person that's leading us is going to lead us right but that's not always the case. We have been put in the position to only hope and pray that the person that is leading us will do the right thing.

We tend to look at colors, we tend to look at faces, we tend to judge everything when it comes to a person of power. With God there's no color, there's no face, there's no religion, there's nothing unless God is leading the person of power. When it's said and done, Christians must hold up the name of God because of the bad positions that we are put in in this life.

Spiritually, as Christians we do have power. We have the authority. We have a say because we are who we say we are. Sometimes we find ourselves having to pray just as hard as others to adapt to whatever situations are going on in this world. The Power that God gave us it was not meant to use people, it was meant to help us. It was meant to give us that **now faith** assurance that which keeps us grounded.

Power is a good thing. it's not made for the negative. This doesn't mean everyone on this Earth has it. It does not mean that Power only belongs to Christians. Power is easy for man to obtain because of who they are rather than who they are spiritually. As Christians, our power goes together with our faith and beliefs that God has led us to obtain.

God gives us power in normal things like having a family (raising our children), maintaining our financial situations, and the power to make our own decisions. As a Christian, you oversee maintaining your power in a spiritual way. God chose me to be a Bishop. I have the power to run different churches in different parts of this world. I have to make sure that I'm leading my flock in a very positive manner. I'm responsible for whomever comes under me. I must lead them in the proper way of the Holy Spirit. Yes, this is a hard thing to do but I was chosen. In my heart and soul, God directs me to do such a job. Do I have the authority to mislead? Yes, everyone does. In my position, knowing God, knowing the fruits of my labor, and my commitment; it's a no-brainer. I am who the Lord wants me to be. I cannot make mistakes, I cannot fall short, I must do according to the word of God and so do you.

On my journey of being the Bishop, there are things that I'm learning more of every day. I try often not to fall short of what God expects me to do when I am leading the People of my congregations. I use my learning tools. Sometimes I find that I fall short of expectations, or that I may need more guidance on various things, but he guides me. He has granted me the power and authority to do so. I'm constantly mentoring and showing people HIS way so that they can have eternal life! That's the power that God has given to me. I must be that example for the people that are around me everyday of my life.

Your power comes from faith. Your power comes from believing and your power comes from enduring every obstacle in your life. Your power is not to be used in a worldly way. When I say worldly, I mean not for your own personal satisfactions that mean nothing to the Lord.

One thing we have to understand is that power is POWER and it is huge. You must use your power very wisely. Everyone has it! Its best used for Spiritual convenience and our rights to lead people to Christ.

The Power of God does not discriminate. Your sons and your daughters shall have prophesy. Old men dream. Young men will have visions. (Acts 2:17)

"He gives strength to the weary and increases the power of the weak" (Isaiah 40:29). The subject of power is very biblical. We must use it with the guidance of our father.

ENDURANCE

What is endurance? Endurance is to suffer (something painful or difficult) patiently. Endurance is also the power to withstand something challenging. It can be used to describe the physical strength to keep going, as in a marathon, or giving birth, but also can be used when discussing an exhausting mental situation or stressful time such as the endurance to bounce back from heartbreak.

"More than that, we rejoice in our suffering, knowing that suffering produces endurance, and endurance produces character, and character produces hope. (Romans 5:3-5)

In the Bible, only Caleb and Joshua advised the Hebrews to proceed immediately to take the land. For his faith Caleb was awarded with a promise from God that he and his descendants should possess it. (Numbers 13-14) Caleb was a descendant of Judah. Joshua and Caleb were spies so to speak. They didn't go with the majority and tried to convince the people of Israel that they can conquer the land.

Caleb silenced the people before Moses and said, "we should go up and take possession of the land and we can absolutely do it." (Numbers 13:30)

Caleb went into the promised Land with Joshua and fought with him for five years. His plans were to take the mountain and run out the people who were the current inhabitants. He went there with 12 spies and he returned with Joshua confident that he could take the land of Canaan. With the strength to endure, through God, Caleb knew he had to act on all of these things. I know we're not asked to take down and conquer a land, but we are expected to act accordingly in the world that the Lord has put before us.

As I mentioned earlier, I spoke of pregnancy from women. When women are in labor, at some point during this life changing ordeal, they decide, "I'm not doing this!" They have to endure through all of the complications until the blessing they received from God is complete, good or bad. That's endurance.

When you are going through a terrible heartbreak, you must find some way to fill that void. The void to fill is not from man. Although, God may send you various people along the way. We must be steadfast and immovable, so we can be guided. With heartbreak, it seems like it's never going to subside. It truly will. We have to trust God and be humble, so he has authority over that particular trial.

In life there are many tests that come along, I mean very hard obstacles. We cannot sit moping around and let the enemy take over. We must be obedient to the knowledge that God has put before us.

After dealing with heartbreak, sometimes we think, "the next person I meet is the one." After such an emotional situation, you have to learn to know yourself in order to carry on. If you are not ready and you don't love yourself, how do you expect someone else to know or understand you as a person. It is the simple things that we sometimes may have to endure.

I have to share with you this story about a house that I was building. If anything could go wrong, it did. I needed to lay the foundation to one of my homes on my own, so my wife and I took on the challenge. First it was the rain. Then it was the trees, they all had to be cut down (by the roots). Finally, I got I was able to begin work on the foundation. Now, it was time to pour the concrete. Except, we couldn't do that because it rained repeatedly. A job that could have been done in days, took me two almost three months.

I said, "God, help me." I needed the endurance to complete this house and I was a bit defeated. I knew this was a time that I would have to have faith in God and him alone.

One day I woke up and looked at the forecast. God said, "this is your day." Not only did I get the concrete laid, I was able to even get more stuff accomplished. I had to have endurance, or I would have failed. I'm only giving you the shortcut version of this job. It was a long drawn out process that my wife and I experienced. I'm telling you, God gives you that physical and mental help when you need it! That's a promise!

FINANCES

How can we acquire wealth? How can I be more financially secure?

"But thou shalt remember the Lord, thy God, for it is he that giveth thee power to get wealth, that he may establish his covenant which he sware unto thy fathers, as it is this day. (Deuteronomy 8:18)

A wise person opened me up to ways of obtaining financial stability. First, you have to save your money. Meaning when you are working, put something back.

For instance, you're making $500.00 per week. Your monthly bills total to $850.00. Of that money, how much can you afford to put up in one month? You average $2000.00 per month. If you are tithing correctly, that means you should have $950.00 for food and recreation. Even if you are only able to set aside $50.00 out of the month, you've taken the first step.

In order to be financially stable, you must be mindful of the money you spend. What about a rainy day? I don't mean rain literally. When things come up unexpectedly, like a medical emergency, or you're replaced from your job, will you be ready for that storm? Do not leave it up to chance. Do not choose to be in a financial rut.

Think of the storms and fires in stock and real estate that the world has came up against lately, were those people prepared for that? These were overwhelming circumstances for people. How many of those victims look back and thought about another financial option they could have taken. It's tough. Most of us rob Peter to pay Paul and live on a very narrow edge. Some of us are living from paycheck to paycheck, but we all have the same options. Some of us will continue education to get a better position. It proves the go getter is always running toward something. This is the same for the people that are in knowledge of Christ and those that seek help from God on a continuous basis.

God provides knowledge and faith on your finances too. Earlier, I mentioned tithing. Are you a tithe giver?

Then Jacob made a vow, saying, "If God will be with me and will keep me in this way that I go, and will give me bread to eat and clothing to wear, so that I come again to my father's house in peace, then shall the Lord be my God: And this stone which I have set up for pillar, shall be God's house. And of all that you will give me I will give a full tenth to you." (Genesis 28:20-22)

Tithes are most important to God. We must give back to Him. If you don't have a church home drop your tithes to a friend or a member of another church but PAY YOUR TITHES!

If you want to gain financially, the Lord requires just 10%. People share a lot of abundant blessings by tithing, ask a faithful tithe payer. It really works, l am a witness.

What people need to know, the more that you give, the more that you receive. Don't you see people around you that are prosperous? It's because they give. They don't just give to the church. They give to different charities, fundraisers, the whole nine yards just to know God is there, and they will never need anything. It's in the Bible

IF YOU WAKE UP YOU CAN CHANGE IT!

I pray and ask God to give back to each of you what the enemy has stolen from you and your families. There is a God! I only ask that as people of God to claim your atmosphere and your God given gifts. I pray that we all change our minds to be more positive. God is not done working on you. We are who we say we are and there is a God. Even when the enemy tries to convince you otherwise. God gave us the strength to endure.

Lord, decrease the negativity and increase the positive in our lives. Lord give your people an increase on their finances and grant us with multiple blessings. As we sleep tonight, please make us over in your likeness. So, remember, if you wake up, you can change it. In Jesus name we pray, amen.

God Bless You

Bishop Alvin Freeman

Printed in the United States
By Bookmasters